# What Can You Hear?

I can hear a cat sip.

4

I can hear a bag rip.

I can hear the rain pit pat.

I can hear a bat flap.

I can hear an owl hoot.

I can hear a trumpet toot.

Toot!

Toot!

I can hear a bird sing.

I can hear a bell ring.

11

I can hear a bubble pop.

12

I can hear a horse clip clop.

13

I can hear a clock tick.

I can hear a lock click.

15

I can hear bees buzz and land.

I can hear boys clap hands.

17

I can hear the pans clang.

We can hear a lot of bangs!

19

# Your Turn

## Match it!

Follow the line from each picture
to read the word.

bell  owl  horse  bubble

# Clap it!

Say the 'Match it!' words.
Clap the syllables.

# Sound it!

Sound out each of these words.

| h ear | b u zz | r ai n | c l a ng |

# Say it!

Read and say these words.

| the | I | of | we |

# Describe it!

cat    lion

hen    snake

1) What sound do these animals make? Can a friend guess which animal you're describing?

2) Some sounds can make us feel happy.
Which sounds make you feel happy?
There are sounds we don't like too.
Which sounds don't you like?

# Do it!

Go on a listening walk.
How many different sounds
can you hear?

# Find it!

Look back in the book and find each of these.

a quiet
sound

a loud
sound

something
that goes
toot

something
that goes
clang

# Notes for Parents and Teachers

Children naturally practise their literacy skills as they discover the world around them. The topics in the **QED Essentials** series help children use these developing skills and broaden their knowledge and vocabulary. Once they have finished reading the text, encourage your child to demonstrate their understanding by having a go at the activities on pages 20–23.

## Reading Tips

•Sit next to your child and let them turn the pages themselves.

•Look through the book before you start reading together. Discuss what you can see on the cover first.

•Encourage your child to use a finger to track the text as they read.

•Keep reading and talking sessions short and at a time that works for both of you. Try to make it a relaxing moment to share with your child.

•Prompt your child to use the picture clues to support their reading when they come across unfamiliar words.

•Give lots of praise as your child reads and return to the book as often as you can. Re-reading leads to greater confidence and fluency.

•Remind your child to use their letter sound knowledge to work out new words.

•Use the 'Your Turn' pages to practise reading new words and to encourage your child to talk about the text.

I can hear a clock tick.

I can hear a lock click.

Colourful photographs open up further discussion points

Short, decodable sentences repeat topic words and commonly used words

Wide range of vocabulary to explore in context

14

15